ARIZONA

A Postcard Book

Photography by Eric Wunrow

FALCON®

Copyright © 1995 by Falcon® Publishing, Inc., Helena, Montana.

All rights reserved. The right to reproduce any part of this book in any form, including photocopying or artistic duplication of photos, is prohibited without written permission from the publisher.

Design, typesetting, and other composition work by Falcon® Publishing, Inc., Helena, Montana.
Printed in Korea.

ISBN 1-56044-322-7

Falcon Press publishes a wide variety of books and calendars. For a free catalog write Falcon, P.O. Box 1718, Helena, Montana 59624, or call toll-free 1-800-582-2665.

Front cover: Sunset and Saguaro, Organ Pipe Cactus National Monument

These slightly oversized postcards require first-class postage.

ARIZONA

Grand Canyon GRAND CANYON NATIONAL PARK

Shadows play in the rugged depths of Grand Canyon National Park. The canyon is nearly three hundred miles long and averages ten miles wide and is one of the few natural land formations visible from space.

Copyright © 1995 Falcon Press.® All Rights Reserved.

PHOTO BY ERIC WUNROW

ARIZONA

Petroglyphs WUPATKI NATIONAL MONUMENT

Petroglyphs remain long after the cultures who etched them are gone. These drawings are only one example of nearly 2,700 archeological sites found in Wupatki National Monument.

Copyright © 1995 Falcon Press ® All Rights Reserved.

PHOTO BY ERIC WUNROW

ARIZONA

Saguaros at Sunset ORGAN PIPE CACTUS NATIONAL MONUMENT

A full palette of colors paints the evening sky over Organ Pipe Cactus National Monument. Sprawling across 516 square miles along the Mexican border, the monument preserves one of the last great expanses of pristine Sonoran Desert in the United States.

Copyright © 1995 Falcon Press.® All Rights Reserved.

PHOTO BY ERIC WUNROW

ARIZONA

Havasu Falls HAVASUPAI INDIAN RESERVATION

Crystal clear waters cascade over Havasu Falls to travertine ledges below. The falls is one of several in Havasu Canyon and is the most popular on the Havasupai Indian Reservation.

Copyright © 1995 Falcon Press.® All Rights Reserved.

PHOTO BY ERIC WUNROW

ARIZONA

Tsegi Canyon NAVAJO NATIONAL MONUMENT

One can almost hear the drums of ancient Anasazi still echoing through the canyons of Navajo National Monument. The 360-acre monument preserves three cliff dwellings believed to have been built by the ancestors of the Hopi Indians in the 15th century.

Copyright © 1995 Falcon Press.® All Rights Reserved.

PHOTO BY ERIC WUNROW

ARIZONA

Petrified Logs PETRIFIED FOREST NATIONAL PARK

The desolate landscape of Petrified Forest National Park is home to a hidden 225 million-year-old forest. Arizona was once in the tropics with trees towering 200 feet above a lush forest floor.

Copyright © 1995 Falcon Press.® All Rights Reserved.

PHOTO BY ERIC WUNROW

A R I Z O N A

Cholla Cactus ORGAN PIPE CACTUS NATIONAL MONUMENT

Pretty to look at, but not to hold; the jumping cholla cactus is not as soft as it appears. The fuzzy joints readily break off when brushed against, embedding sharp spines in their new host.

Copyright © 1995 Falcon Press.® All Rights Reserved.

PHOTO BY ERIC WUNROW

ARIZONA

Spider Rock CANYON DE CHELLY NATIONAL MONUMENT

Spider Rock, called Tse Na'ashje'ii by the Navajo, is the world's tallest free-standing spire. Local legend has it that the spire is home to Na'ashje'ii Asdzaa, or Spider Woman, an important deity in the Navajo pantheon.

Copyright © 1995 Falcon Press.® All Rights Reserved.

PHOTO BY ERIC WUNROW

A R I Z O N A

Fresh Snow on Autumn Leaves   TONTO NATIONAL FOREST

Fresh snow accompanies the dazzling colors of fall in the Sierra Ancha Mountains of Tonto National Forest. Aspen groves are abundant in the coniferous forests that cover ten percent of Arizona's landscape.

Copyright © 1995 Falcon Press.® All Rights Reserved.

PHOTO BY ERIC WUNROW

A R I Z O N A

Sandstone Patterns UPPER ANTELOPE CANYON

Only patterns remain where water once flowed. Upper Antelope Canyon is considered by many to be the most beautiful slot canyon in the country. The varying colors of red, orange, purple, and brown are due to iron oxides in the sand.

Copyright © 1995 Falcon Press.® All Rights Reserved.

PHOTO BY ERIC WUNROW

ARIZONA

Monument Valley MONUMENT VALLEY TRIBAL PARK

Cooling breezes and the warm glow of the setting sun suffuse Monument Valley with a golden inner glow: The end of another perfect day in Arizona.

Copyright © 1995 Falcon Press.® All Rights Reserved.

Photo by Eric Wunrow

A R I Z O N A

Saguaro Cactus in Fog WHITE TANKS REGIONAL PARK

Morning sun lifts a blanket of fog from White Tanks Regional Park, revealing the desert below. Saguaro cactus like these may be two centuries old. A mature saguaro can reach 50 feet high and weigh nearly ten tons.

Copyright © 1995 Falcon Press.® All Rights Reserved.

PHOTO BY ERIC WUNROW

ARIZONA

Lake Powell and Mesas GLEN CANYON NATIONAL RECREATION AREA

Beautiful mesas hold back the waters of Lake Powell in Glen Canyon National Recreation Area. With nearly 2,000 miles of shoreline, Lake Powell is the second largest manmade reservoir in the world.

Copyright © 1995 Falcon Press.® All Rights Reserved.

PHOTO BY ERIC WUNROW

ARIZONA

Grand Canyon GRAND CANYON NATIONAL PARK

Darkness envelops the Grand Canyon as the last rays of daylight fade away. One thousand feet higher than the South Rim, the North Rim receives twice as much precipitation, including 140 inches of snow annually.

Copyright © 1995 Falcon Press.® All Rights Reserved.

PHOTO BY ERIC WUNROW

A R I Z O N A

Petrified Log PETRIFIED FOREST NATIONAL PARK

You can still count the rings in this log in Petrified Forest National Park. According to Navajo legend, the logs found in the park are the bones of Yietso, an ancient monster slain by ancestral Navajos.

Copyright © 1995 Falcon Press.® All Rights Reserved.

PHOTO BY ERIC WUNROW

ARIZONA

Organ Pipe Cactus & Ajo Mountains ORGAN PIPE CACTUS NATIONAL MONUMENT

The rugged Ajo range in Organ Pipe Cactus National Monument provides a grand backdrop for the park's namesake. These stately cactus can reach heights of 20 feet and bear fruit that is collected by Papago Indians for syrup and winter food.

Copyright © 1995 Falcon Press.® All Rights Reserved.

PHOTO BY ERIC WUNROW

ARIZONA

Hohokam Petroglyphs SAGUARO NATIONAL PARK

Surprises can be found around every corner in Arizona's newest national park. Saguaro National Park was once home to the Hohokam tribe between A.D. 900–1300. Petroglyphs and other artifacts are all that remain of these ancient people.

Copyright © 1995 Falcon Press.® All Rights Reserved.

PHOTO BY ERIC WUNROW

ARIZONA

Red Rock Crossing OAK CREEK CANYON

First light brings dark shadows to Red Rock Crossing in Oak Creek Canyon. Driving the canyon is an exhilarating experience. The road clings to canyon sides as the sunset-colored buttes jut up out of the desert that stretches ahead.

Copyright © 1995 Falcon Press.® All Rights Reserved.

PHOTO BY ERIC WUNROW

ARIZONA

Painted Desert PETRIFIED FOREST NATIONAL PARK

Colors change before your eyes at the Painted Desert in Petrified Forest National Park. The multicolored shades of purple, red, brown, gray, and green change with sunlight between dawn and dusk. The formations are colored by iron oxides in the soil.

Copyright © 1995 Falcon Press.® All Rights Reserved.

PHOTO BY ERIC WUNROW

A R I Z O N A

DISCOVER ARIZONA

There's no time like the present to get out
and sample Arizona's recreational opportunities.

LET FALCON BE YOUR GUIDE.

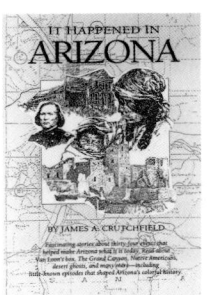   

For a free catalog of books, maps, and other Arizona products,
please return this card with the following information:

Name: _____

Address: _____

City: _____ State: _____ Zip: _____

Or call **1-800-582-2665**

FALCON™

BUSINESS REPLY MAIL
FIRST-CLASS MAIL PERMIT NO 80 HELENA MT

POSTAGE WILL BE PAID BY ADDRESSEE

FALCON™
PO BOX 1718
HELENA MT 59624-9948